I AM A GOOD DIGITAL CITIZEN

I AM
SMART
ONLINE

RACHAEL MORLOCK

PowerKiDS press.

NEW YORK

Published in 2020 by The Rosen Publishing Group, Inc.
29 East 21st Street, New York, NY 10010

First Edition

Editor: Elizabeth Krajnik
Book Design: Reann Nye

Photo Credits: Cover PR Image Factory/Shutterstock.com; p. 5 Patrick Foto/Shutterstock.com; p. 7 Rido/Shutterstock.com; p. 9 goodluz/Shutterstock.com; p. 11 Rawpixel.com/Shutterstock.com; p. 13 Branislav Nenin/Shutterstock.com; p. 15 Sharaf Maksumov/Shutterstock.com; p. 17 Sergey Maksienko/Shutterstock.com; p. 19 Ollyy/Shutterstock.com; p. 21 Monkey Business Images/Shutterstock.com; p. 22 GagliardiImages/Shutterstock.com.

Cataloging-in-Publication Data

Names: Morlock, Rachael.
Title: I am smart online / Rachael Morlock.
Description: New York : PowerKids Press, 2020. | Series: I am a good digital citizen | Includes glossary and index.
Identifiers: ISBN 9781538349687 (pbk.) | ISBN 9781538349700 (library bound) | ISBN 9781538349694 (6pack)
Subjects: LCSH: Internet and children–Juvenile literature. | Internet–Safety measures–Juvenile literature.
Classification: LCC HQ784.I58 M673 2020 | DDC 004.67'80289–dc23

Manufactured in the United States of America

CPSIA Compliance Information: Batch #CSPK19. For Further Information contact Rosen Publishing, New York, New York at 1-800-237-9932.

CONTENTS

ONE IN A BILLION 4

BE SMART! 6

KNOW THE RULES 8

SMART SEARCHES 10

TRUSTWORTHY WEBSITES 14

FACT OR OPINION? 16

CHECK YOUR FACTS 18

STAY ORGANIZED 20

KEEP LEARNING! 22

GLOSSARY 23

INDEX 24

WEBSITES 24

ONE IN A BILLION

When you're at home, you're a family member. When you're at school, you're a student. When you're playing a sport, you're a teammate. But what are you when you go online? You're a digital citizen! Billions of people across the world use the Internet. That makes them digital citizens, too.

BE SMART!

You can practice good digital citizenship by being fair, respectful, and smart online. Smart digital citizens are ready to learn about the Internet by trying new things and asking for help. They learn how to find trustworthy websites. Most importantly, they are thoughtful about what they look at and do online.

KNOW THE RULES

Smart digital citizens follow rules to keep themselves and others safe. Some rules are for everyone. Your school may have special rules for students, and your family may have special rules just for you. Once you know the rules, the Internet is a great tool for finding **information**.

SMART SEARCHES

How do you search for information online? The Internet is huge! It can be hard to find exactly what you're looking for. But there are ways to make your searches smarter. Use more than one **term** to help narrow down your search, and always make sure your spelling is **correct**.

Let's say you're looking for facts about *T. rex*. First, choose a **search engine**. Next, type your terms into the search bar. Instead of searching for "T. rex," try "T. rex dinosaur." Once you've found helpful websites, you can use them again.

T. rex dinosaur

13

TRUSTWORTHY WEBSITES

Trustworthy websites give you facts that you can count on. When you search for facts online, look for websites that end in ".gov," ".org," or ".edu." These endings mean the government, **organizations**, or schools created those websites. Often, these sites have **expert** knowledge you can trust.

.gov | Cit... ✕   +

🔒 https://www1.nyc.gov

bsite of the City of New York

YC Resources   NYC311   Office o

15

FACT OR OPINION?

Can you tell the difference between facts and opinions? A fact is something that can be proven. An opinion is a belief or feeling about something. Some websites are more likely to share facts, while others share only opinions. For example, a **blog** is usually a website for sharing opinions.

CHECK YOUR FACTS

Once you've found information you think is factual, there are ways to make sure it's true. Even trusted websites make mistakes sometimes. It's always smart to check your facts. See if you can find the same fact on three trustworthy websites. You can also check in a book or ask an adult if you're not sure.

STAY ORGANIZED

Keep track of the websites you use. Take notes about where you find information. If you're using your own computer, you can bookmark websites so you can find them again later and give them **credit**. If you're writing a paper, make sure you keep track of the websites you use as you go.

KEEP LEARNING!

Being a smart digital citizen doesn't mean knowing everything about the Internet! The Internet is huge, and it's always changing and growing. Being a smart digital citizen means learning from your mistakes and successes online. It means thinking carefully about what you find on the Internet and how you can use that information.

GLOSSARY

blog: A website on which someone writes about personal opinions, activities, and experiences.

correct: Free from mistakes.

credit: Recognition or honor received for some quality or work.

expert: Showing special skill or knowledge gained from experience or training.

information: Knowledge or facts about something.

organization: A group formed for a specific purpose.

search engine: A website or software used to search data for requested information.

term: A word or phrase that has an exact meaning.

INDEX

B
blog, 16

C
computer, 20
credit, 20

F
facts, 12, 14, 16, 18
family, 4, 8

G
government, 14

H
help, 6

I
information, 8, 10, 18, 20, 22
Internet, 4, 6, 8, 10, 22

K
knowledge, 14

M
mistakes, 18, 22

O
opinions, 16
organizations, 14

R
rules, 8

S
school, 4, 8, 14
search, 10, 12
search engine, 12
spelling, 10

T
term, 10

W
websites, 6, 12, 14, 16, 18, 20

WEBSITES

Due to the changing nature of Internet links, PowerKids Press has developed an online list of websites related to the subject of this book. This site is updated regularly. Please use this link to access the list: www.powerkidslinks.com/digcit/smart